A Victorian Christmas

Edited by
Evelyn Beilenson

Design by
Michel Design

PETER PAUPER PRESS, INC.
WHITE PLAINS · NEW YORK

To Larry

Copyright © 1990
Peter Pauper Press, Inc.
202 Mamaroneck Avenue
White Plains, New York 10601
ISBN 0-88088-034-1
Library of Congress No. 90-61143
Printed in the United States of America
5   4   3   2   1

CONTENTS

INTRODUCTION

A Victorian Christmas conjures up delightful scenes of family gatherings, sumptuous meals, lantern-lit carolers wrapped in warm winter cloaks and scarves, beautifully illustrated lacy cards, and trees decorated with hundreds of candles and homemade ornaments.

Our love of nostalgia at this particular time of year transports us naturally to the reign of Queen Victoria (1837-1901).

Victorians tried especially at Christmas to emulate the manner in which their beloved queen celebrated the holiday. She had an enormous influence on her people, who followed her example from Christmas Eve to Boxing Day.

It is apparent in Victorian art, Victorian music, and especially in Victorian literature that the people of the 19th Century in every part of the world loved Christmas.

An excerpt from Princess Victoria's diary dated December 24, 1832, when she was 13 years old, allows the reader a glimpse of Victoria's Christmas as a child. This is a natural introduction to the customs, foods, songs, and literature of a Victorian Christmas:

After dinner we went upstairs. I then saw Flora, the dog which Sir John was going to give Mamma. Aunt Sophia came also. We then went into the drawing room near the dining room. After Mamma had rung a bell three times we went in. There were two large round tables on which were placed two trees hung with lights and sugar ornaments. All the presents being placed round the tree.

I had one table for myself and the Conroy family had the other together. Lehzen had likewise a little table. Mamma gave me a little lovely pink bag which she had worked with a little sachet likewise done by her; a beautiful little opal brooch and earrings, books, some lovely prints, a pink satin dress and a cloak lined with fur. Aunt Sophia gave me a dress which she worked herself, and Aunt Mary a pair of amethyst earrings. Lehzen a lovely music-book. Victoire a pretty white bag worked by herself, and Sir John a silver brush . . .

Mamma then took me up into my bedroom with all the ladies. There was a new toilet table with a white muslin cover over pink and all my silver things standing on it with a fine new looking-glass. I stayed up till half past 9.

CHRISTMAS FARE

At the time that Queen Victoria ascended to the throne (1837) a traditional Christmas dinner included roast beef (in the North of England) or goose (in the South). Other dishes might have been peacock, turtle soup, oyster patties, mashed potatoes, suckling pig, boar, port jelly, and, of course, plum pudding and mince pies.

In America, turkey was substituted for roast peacock. Ham did not replace suckling pig until the late 1800's. Back in England, roast turkey did not appear on the Royal Christmas Day menu until 1851.

Charles Dickens' *A Christmas Carol* regales us with Scrooge's delight at waking up on Christmas Day and discovering that all was a bad dream. His personality has taken a drastic change for the better when he calls a boy loitering outside his house to fetch him a turkey:

"Do you know the Poulterer's, in the next street but one, at the corner?" Scrooge inquired.

"I should hope I did," replied the lad.

"An intelligent boy!" said Scrooge. "A remarkable boy! Do you know whether they've sold the prize Turkey that was hanging up there? —Not the little prize Turkey, the big one?"

"What, the one as big as me?" returned the boy.

"What a delightful boy!" said Scrooge.

"It's a pleasure to talk to him. Yes, my buck!" "It's hanging there now," replied the boy.

"It is?" said Scrooge. "Go and buy it."

"Walk-er!" exclaimed the boy.

"No, no," said Scrooge, "I am in earnest. Go and buy it, and tell 'em to bring it here, that I may give them the direction where to take it. Come back with the man, and I'll give you a shilling. Come back with him in less than five minutes, and I'll give you a half a crown!"

The boy was off like a shot. He must have had a steady hand at a trigger who could have got a shot off half so fast.

"I'll send it to Bob Cratchit's!"

Recipes for turkey, stuffing (definitely an English import), roast beef, roast goose, baked Virginia ham, English plum pudding, hard sauce and mince pie follow. Recipes in italics are original recipes from the 19th Century with the modern-day versions in roman.

Turkey Roast

TO ROAST A TURKEY—Make a stuffing like that for veal; or take a tea cup of Sausage meat and add a like quantity of bread crumbs, with the beaten yolk of two eggs—then fill the crop; dredge the turkey over with flour, lay it before the fire, taking care this is most on the stuffed part, as that requires the greatest heat. A strip of paper may be put on the breast bone to prevent its scorching. Baste with a little butter or salt and water at first, then with its own drippings. A little before it is taken up, dredge it again with flour, baste with butter and froth it up. A larger turkey (8 lbs) requires full three hours roasting—a smaller one in proportion. (Ham or tongue is usually eaten with turkey; stewed cranberries also.)

The Way to Live Well and
Be Well While We Live,
by Mrs. S. J. Hale, 1839

11

Roast Turkey

Dress and clean turkey. Rub inside with salt and pepper. Stuff neck cavity. Fasten opening with metal pins. Fill body cavity loosely with stuffing. Rub with butter or make paste of ½ cup butter, ¾ cup flour; spread over all parts of the turkey.

Place turkey breast side down in open roasting pan to allow juices to run down into breast. Drip pan from broiler may be used if large roaster is not available. Roast uncovered in 300° to 325° oven 15 to 20 minutes per pound, turning turkey over onto back when half done.

Baste at 30-minute intervals with mixture of melted butter and hot water. When breast and legs become light brown, cover with brown paper. Turkey is done when the meat pulls away from the leg-bones.

Roast Goose

Singe, remove pin feathers, then wash in cold water and wipe. Sprinkle with salt and pepper. Stuff with bread stuffing. Place breast side up on rack in roasting pan.

Pour 2 cups boiling water over and cover.
Roast 25 to 30 minutes per pound in
moderately slow oven (325° to 350°),
basting with fat every 15 minutes. When
goose is done, garnish with cranberries and
watercress, and serve with apple sauce.

Stuffing

A good stuffing for veal, mutton or poultry:
Take two cups of bread crumbs and one of
butter or minced suet, a little parsley, finely
shredded, one quarter of a nutmeg grated, a
tea-spoonful of powdered lemon peel, allspice,
and salt—the whole to be worked together with
two or three yolks of egg, well beat.

> The Way to Live Well and
> Be Well While We Live,
> *by Mrs. S. J. Hale, 1839*

Stuffing

¾   cup ground pork
1   tablespoon powdered sage
1   tablespoon salt
1   teaspoon pepper
¾   cup bread crumbs (rye or whole wheat)
2   egg yolks, beaten

Blend pork, sage, salt, and pepper. Mix with bread crumbs. Add beaten egg yolks and mix thoroughly.

Baked Virginia Ham

Place ham fat side up on rack in open roasting pan. Add ⅓″ water to pan. Do not cover. Bake in 350° oven, allowing 20 minutes per pound for a large ham; 25 minutes per pound for a small ham; and 30 minutes per pound for a half ham. Roast meat thermometer registers 170° when ham is done. Ham may be basted during cooking period with ginger ale or cider. For the last half hour of baking, rub surface with mustard and brown sugar. Score fat in diamonds; stick a whole clove in each.

Standing Rib Roast

Select a 2-rib or 3-rib standing rib roast (4 to 5 pounds). Place fat side up in roasting pan; season with salt and pepper and place in 350° oven. Do not cover and do not add water.

Allow 18 to 20 minutes per pound for rare roasts, 22 to 25 minutes per pound for medium, and 27 to 30 minutes per pound for well-done roasts. Serve with Yorkshire Pudding.

English Plum Pudding

10   slices white bread
1   cup scalded milk

½   cup sugar
4   eggs, separated
1⅓ cups golden raisins, lightly floured
½   cup finely chopped dates
3   tablespoons finely chopped citron
¾   cup finely chopped suet
3   tablespoons brandy (optional)
1   teaspoon nutmeg
½   teaspoon cinnamon
¼   teaspoon ground cloves
¼   teaspoon mace
1   teaspoon salt

Crumb bread and soak in hot milk. Cool
and add sugar, egg yolks, raisins, dates, and
citron. Cream suet in food processor and
add to crumb mixture. Stir in brandy (if
desired), nutmeg, cinnamon, cloves, mace,
and salt. Beat until well blended. Beat egg
whites until stiff but not dry. Stir a third of
the egg whites into pudding mixture; gently
fold in the remainder. Spoon mixture into a
buttered 2-quart mold and cover. Steam for
6 hours in a large covered pot holding
boiling water to come halfway up the sides
of the mold. Remove and let cool for 10
minutes before unmolding. Serve with
warm hard sauce.

Hard Sauce

5   tablespoons butter
1   cup confectioners sugar
½   teaspoon vanilla

Cream butter, add sugar and beat with
electric beater until pale and creamy. Add
vanilla and blend. Cover and refrigerate
until needed.

Mince Pies

*Ingredients for mincemeat:—One and a half
pounds of lean underdone roast beef, two
pounds of beef suet, one pound of stoned
raisins, one pound of picked sultanas, one and
a half pounds of apples, one and a half
pounds of pears, one pound of mixed peel,
three quarters of a pound of blanched and*

chopped Valencia almonds, the thin peel of two oranges and two lemons. All the before-mentioned ingredients are to be chopped and then mixed with one pound of well washed and dried currants, a quarter of an ounce of mixed powdered spice, the juice from the lemons and oranges, one and a half pounds of Demerara sugar, half a pint of brandy, half a pint of sherry, half a pint of port, one wineglassful each of Marshall's maraschino syrup and noyeau syrup, and a quarter of a pint of Silver Rays (white) rum.

Make some puff paste, roll it out a quarter of an inch thick, and line some little plain or fancy pattypans with it; place a teaspoonful or dessertspoonful, or more, of mincemeat in each, according to its size, wet the edges of the paste and cover the mincemeat over with more paste; brush over the top with beaten-up whole raw egg, and put them in a quick oven for about five minutes, then take them out, dust them over with icing sugar to glaze them, and put them back to bake for fifteen to twenty minutes. Dish up in a pile on a dishpaper or napkin, and serve hot.

from Mrs. Agnes B. Marshall's
cook book from the
early Victorian period

Mincemeat Pie

1   can (1⅔ cups) mincemeat
2   cups thinly sliced apples
1   teaspoon grated lemon peel
2   tablespoons lemon juice
      Pastry dough for 9-inch 2-crust pie

Combine mincemeat, apples, lemon peel, and juice; heat thoroughly. Pour into 9-inch pastry-lined pie pan; adjust top crust. Sprinkle with a small amount of sugar and bake in 400° oven 35 minutes.

After dinner in Victorian times, a large silver wassail bowl was brought in to warm the spirits of friends, family, and carolers, or wassailers, who happened to come by. These wassailers were sometimes served a glass of punch and a piece of mince pie.

In *Old Christmas,* Washington Irving describes the festivities that occurred when the wassail bowl was brought to the table:

When the cloth was removed, the butler brought in a huge silver vessel, of rare and curious workmanship, which he placed before the 'Squire. Its appearance was hailed with acclamation; being the Wassail Bowl, so renowned in Christmas festivity. The contents had been prepared by the 'Squire himself; for it was a beverage, in the skillful mixture of which he particularly prided himself: alleging that it was too abstruse and complex for the comprehension of an ordinary servant. It was a potation, indeed, that might well make the heart of a toper leap within him; being composed of the richest and raciest wines, highly spiced and sweetened, with roasted apples bobbing about the surface.

The old gentleman's whole countenance beamed with a serene look of indwelling delight, as he stirred his mighty bowl. Having raised it to his lips, with a hearty wish of a merry Christmas to all present, he sent it brimming around the board, for every one to follow his example according to the primitive style; pronouncing it "the ancient fountain of good feeling, where all hearts met together."

In Merrie Old England the wassail bowl was sometimes made with ale instead of wine or cider, with nutmeg, sugar, toast, ginger and roasted apples. Thick cream was sometimes added. The pieces of toast floated on top— the origin of the drinking "toast." The nut-brown beverage is still prepared this way in some traditional families.

The following is a modern-day version of this wonderful hearty punch:

Punch

1	quart cider
¼	teaspoon cinnamon
4	cloves
¼	teaspoon sugar
6	orange slices
	Nutmeg

Pour cider into a heavy saucepan and add cloves. While heating, add cinnamon, cloves, sugar, and orange slices. Serve with nutmeg sprinkled on top.

CHRISTMAS CAROLS

The wassailers—children and adults—carried their lanterns from house to house while singing old and new carols. Most of the carols we sing today were written or set to music in Victorian times. Some of those were *Hark! the Herald Angels Sing, O Little Town of Bethlehem, Good King Wenceslas,* and *O Come, All Ye Faithful.*

Until the 19th Century, few carols were printed. Thanks to the Victorians who composed, collected, and published these carols, we now have them forever.

We Three Kings of Orient Are

We three kings of Orient are,
Bearing gifts we traverse afar,
Field and fountain, moor and mountain,
Following yonder star. O—

Refrain
Star of wonder, star of night,
Star with royal beauty bright,
Westward leading, still proceeding,
Guide us to thy perfect light.

Glorious now behold Him arise,
King, and God, and sacrifice;
Heaven sings alleluia;
Alleluia the earth replies. O—

Refrain
Star of wonder, star of night,
Star with royal beauty bright,
Westward leading, still proceeding,
Guide us to thy perfect light.

It Came Upon the Midnight Clear

It came upon the midnight clear,
That glorious song of old,
From angels bending near the earth
To touch their harps of gold;
"Peace on the earth, good will to men,
From heav'n's all-gracious King,"
The world in solemn stillness lay
To hear the angels sing.

Still through the cloven skies they come,
With peaceful wings unfurled,
And still their heav'nly music floats
O'er all the weary world;
Above its sad and lowly plains
They bend on hov'ring wing,
And ever o'er its Babel sounds
The blessed angels sing.

Jingle Bells

Dashing through the snow,
In a one-horse open sleigh,
O'er the fields we go,
Laughing all the way;
The bells on bobtail ring,
Making spirits bright,
O what fun it is to sing
A sleighing song tonight!

Jingle bells, jingle bells,
Jingle all the way!
Oh, what fun it is to ride
In a one-horse open sleigh!
Jingle bells, jingle bells,
Jingle all the way!
Oh, what fun it is to ride
In a one-horse open sleigh!

What Child Is This?

What child is this, Who, laid to rest,
On Mary's lap is sleeping?
Whom angels greet with anthems sweet,
While shepherds watch are keeping?

Refrain
This, this is Christ the King,
Whom shepherds guard and angels sing:
This, this who bring Him love
The Babe, the Son of Mary.

Why lies He in such mean estate
Where ox and ass are feeding?
Good Christian, fear: for sinners here
The silent Word is pleading.

Refrain

So bring Him incense, gold, and myrrh,
Come, peasant, king to own Him;
The King of kings salvation brings,
Let loving hearts enthrone him.

Refrain

Hark! The Herald Angels Sing

Hark! the herald angels sing,
"Glory to the newborn King;"
Peace on earth, and mercy mild,
God and sinners reconciled!
Joyful, all ye nations, rise,
Join the triumph of the skies;
With th'angelic hosts proclaim,
"Christ is born in Bethlehem!"

Refrain
Hark! the herald angels sing,
"Glory to the newborn King."

Christ, by highest heaven adored;
Christ, the everlasting Lord;
Late in time behold Him come,
Offspring of the virgin's womb.
Veiled in flesh the Godhead see;
Hail th'Incarnate Deity,
Pleased as man with man to dwell;
Jesus, our Emmanuel.

Refrain

Hail, the heav'n born Prince of Peace!
Hail, the Sun of Righteousness!
Light and life to all He brings,
Ris'n with healing in His wings;
Mild He lays His glory by,
Born that man no more may die,
Born to raise the sons of earth,
Born to give them second birth.

Refrain

O Little Town of Bethlehem

O little town of Bethlehem,
How still we see thee lie!
Above thy deep and dreamless sleep,
The silent stars go by;
Yet in thy dark streets shineth
The everlasting Light;
The hopes and fears of all the years
Are met in thee tonight.

For Christ is born of Mary,
And gathered all above,
While mortals sleep, the angels keep
Their watch of wond'ring love.
O morning stars, together
Proclaim the holy birth,
And praises sing to God the King,
And peace to men on earth!

O holy Child of Bethlehem,
Descend to us, we pray;
Cast out our sin and enter in;
Be born in us today!
We hear the Christmas Angels
The great glad tidings tell;
O come to us, abide with us
Our Lord Emmanuel!

Good King Wenceslas

Good King Wenceslas look'd out,
On the Feast of Stephen,
When the snow lay round about,
Deep, and crisp and even:
Brightly shone the moon that night,
Though the frost was cruel,
When a poor man came in sight,
Gath'ring winter fuel.

"Hither, page, and stand by me,
If thou know'st it, telling,
Yonder peasant, who is he?
Where and what his dwelling?"
"Sire, he lives a good league hence,
Underneath the mountain;
Right against the forest fence,
By Saint Agnes' fountain."

"Bring me flesh, and bring me wine,
Bring me pine-logs hither:
Thou and I will see him dine,
When we bear them thither."
Page and monarch forth they went,
Forth they went together;
Through the rude wind's wild lament
And the bitter weather.

"Sire, the night is darker now,
And the wind blows stronger;
Fails my heart, I know not how,
I can go no longer."
"Mark my footsteps, good my page;
Tread thou in them boldly:
Thou shalt find the winter's rage
Freeze thy blood less coldly."

In his master's steps he trod,
Where the snow lay dinted;
Heat was in the very sod
Which the saint had printed.
Therefore, Christian men, be sure,
Wealth or rank possessing,
Ye who now will bless the poor,
Shall yourselves find blessing.

God Rest You Merry, Gentlemen

God rest you merry, gentlemen,
Let nothing you dismay,
Remember Christ our Saviour
Was born on Christmas Day;
To save us all from Satan's pow'r
When we were gone astray;
O tidings of comfort and joy, comfort and joy,
O tidings of comfort and joy.

In Bethlehem, in Jewry,
This blessed Babe was born,
And laid within a manger,
Upon this blessed Morn;
The which His Mother Mary,
Did nothing take in scorn.
    O tidings, etc.

From God our Heavenly Father,
A blessed Angel came;
And unto certain Shepherds,
Brought tidings of the same:
How that in Bethlehem was born;
The Son of God by Name.
    O tidings, etc.

O Come, All Ye Faithful

O come, all ye faithful, joyful and triumphant,
O come ye, O come ye to Bethlehem;
Come and behold Him, born the King of
    angels;
O come, let us adore Him,
O come, let us adore Him,
O come, let us adore Him, Christ, the Lord!

Sing, choirs of angels, sing in exultation,
O sing, all ye citizens of heaven above!
Glory to God, all glory in the highest;
O come, let us adore Him,
O come, let us adore Him,
O come, let us adore Him, Christ, the Lord!

Yea, Lord, we greet Thee, born this happy
    morning,
Jesus, to Thee be all glory giv'n'
Word of the Father, now in flesh appearing;
O come, let us adore Him,
O come, let us adore Him,
O come, let us adore Him, Christ, the Lord!

CHRISTMAS TREES AND ORNAMENTATION

The marriage of Queen Victoria and Prince Albert united not only two royal families but also the cultures of Britain and Germany. Of the customs Prince Albert introduced to his new home, the Christmas Tree is perhaps the most enduring. In 1841 the royal couple first decorated a table-top tree to the delight of the palace's children *and adults*! In the years to follow, trees quickly became the symbol of the family-oriented tradition of Christmas.

These fir trees, of course, were not left bare, but rather embellished with a wide array of ornaments. The earliest decorations consisted of shiny red apples, strings of popcorn, walnuts painted gold, and barley sugar and other confections. The "edible" quality of the ornamentation led to the custom of calling the tree a "sugartree." When the tree was dismantled on January 5th, the Eve of Epiphany, the sweets would be raffled off to the eager children.

The recipe for one of these yummy ornaments follows:

Yuletide Cookies

½   cup soft butter
½   cup sugar
1   egg
1   tablespoon milk or cream
½   teaspoon vanilla
½   teaspoon lemon extract
1½   cups flour
1   teaspoon cream of tartar
½   teaspoon baking soda
¼   teaspoon salt

Combine ingredients in above order. Chill dough. Roll out to ¼-inch thickness. Cut into fancy shapes with cookie cutters. Sprinkle with colored sugar and bake at 375° on greased cookie sheets until very lightly browned—about 8-10 minutes. Watch carefully to keep from over-browning. One recipe makes about 80 small cookies. If desired, make a hole at the top of each cookie before baking so that cookies my be hung on the tree with a colored ribbon.

The sugary Victorian tree was usually decorated on Christmas Eve and stood only for twelve nights. Thank goodness that custom did not dictate a longer reign for the tree! Lit with wax candles, the tree had to be carefully watched for accidental fires. Buckets of water were often hidden near the tree for just such emergencies. The vigils were worth it, though. The candles gave a shimmering, warm glow to the tree, casting sparkling shadows across the room.

It is little wonder that the fashion of Christmas trees became so popular in Victorian times. In their enthusiasm, the Victorians became avid collectors of much more intricate ornaments, especially the glass balls of Germany. Molded glass figures in different colors could also be obtained, as well as silken sacks (the perfect cache for a sweetmeat!), flags, tiny toys, and gilded angels.

For many families though, invention was the key to Victorian ornamentation. Figures ranging from crocodiles to trolley cars would be cut out of cardboard and embossed with gold or silver on both sides.

Stars and bells would be fashioned from straw soaked in water. Squares of paper could even be rolled into cones and, once decorated, be used as cornucopias to hold comfits and candies. Most creative of the home-made decorations were ornaments called "scraps." These scraps were pieces of paper on which colorful scenes were printed with color lithography. The figures could be cut out and pasted to cardboard, cookies, or cornucopias.

The Victorians trimmed their trees in a singularly festive style with an array of decorations that they either bought or made. Charles Dickens perhaps best describes the experience of the Victorian tree in his 1850 essay, *Household Words:*

I have been looking at a merry company of children assembled round that pretty German toy, a Christmas Tree. The tree was planted in the middle of a great round table, and towered high above their heads. It was brilliantly lighted by a multitude of little tapers; and everywhere sparkled and glittered with bright objects. There were rosy-cheeked dolls, hiding behind the green leaves; and there were real watches (with movable hands, at least, and an endless capacity of being wound up) dangling from innumerable twigs; there were French-polished tables, chairs, bedsteads, wardrobes, eight-day clocks, and various other articles of domestic furniture (wonderfully made in tin), perched among the boughs, as if in preparation for some fairy housekeeping; there were jolly, broadfaced little men, much more agreeable in appearance than many real men—and no wonder, for their heads took off, and showed them to be full of sugar-plums; there were trinkets for the elder girls, far brighter than any grown-up gold and jewels; there were baskets and pincushions in all devices; there were guns, swords, and banners; there were witches standing in enchanted rings of pasteboard, to tell fortunes; there were teetotums, humming-tops, needle-cases, pen-wipers, smelling-bottles, conversation-cards, bouquet-holders; real fruit, made artificially dazzling with gold leaf; imitation apples, pears, and walnuts, crammed with surprises; in short, as a pretty child, before me, delightedly whispered to another pretty child, her bosom friend, "There was everything, and more."

CHRISTMAS CARDS

Christmas cards as we know them today
became popular in the mid-19th Century.
When England, in 1840, adopted the
"penny post," greetings could be sent
almost anywhere in the country for a one-
penny stamp. Prior to this time, the
recipient of the greeting had to pay the
carrier whatever he demanded.

By 1860, companies began producing cards.
These cards looked like valentines, with
ribbon, lace, and poems of love:

> *May thy Christmas*
> *happy be,*
> *And naught*
> *but joy appear,*
> *Is now the wish*
> *I send to thee,*
> *And all I love*
> *most dear.*

Verse on a Victorian
Christmas card

The shapes and sizes of the cards were varied. Most scenes were secular, since card giving was a social rather than a religious custom. The Victorians loved novelty items: pop-up and trick or mechanical cards, scented cards with tassels, and puzzles and jeweled designs were some of the inventive creations of this period.

> *In this festive happy season*
> *Gladness sets the fancy free,*
> *And my thoughts, as swift as swallows,*
> *Fly to bid Good Cheer to thee.*
> Victorian Christmas greeting

CHRISTMAS DECORATIONS

With holly and ivy,
So green and so gay,
We deck up our houses
As fresh as the day;

With bay and rosemary
And laurel complete;
And every one now
Is a king in conceit.

But give me holly, bold and jolly
Honest, prickly, shining holly;
Pluck me holly leaf and berry
For the day when I make merrry.

Christina Rossetti

The Victorians were not the first to decorate their homes with holly, ivy, and mistletoe. But, as with everything else, they did it beautifully and with great enthusiasm.

These charming paragraphs from Dickens' *Christmas with Mr. Pickwick* describe Mr. Pickwick's delight at being kissed under the mistletoe:

Now the screaming had subsided, and faces were in a glow and curls in a tangle, and Mr. Pickwick, after kissing the old lady as beforementioned, was standing under the mistletoe, looking with a very pleased countenance on all that was passing around him, when the young lady with the black eyes, after a little whispering with the other young ladies, made a sudden dart forward, and, putting her arm round Mr. Pickwick's neck, saluted him affectionately on the left cheek; and before Mr. Pickwick distinctly knew what was the matter, he was surrounded by the whole body, and kissed by every one of them.

It was a pleasant thing to see Mr. Pickwick in the centre of the group, now pulled this way, and then that, and first kissed on the chin and then on the nose, and then on the spectacles, and to hear the peals of laughter which were raised on every side.

CHARITABLE WORKS

Christmas has always been a time of giving as well as receiving. Following the tradition of Queen Victoria who distributed well over 2,000 Christmas boxes on Boxing Day, usually the day after Christmas, people would give presents of money and food to the poor and to tradespeople who had served them well during the year. This custom of charitable work was not restricted to England alone, as is well exemplified in Harriet Beecher Stowe's *Christmas; or, The Good Fairy.*

CHRISTMAS; OR, THE GOOD FAIRY

"Oh, dear! Christmas is coming in a fortnight, and I have got to think up presents for everybody!" said young Ellen Stuart, as she leaned languidly back in her chair. "Dear me, it's so tedious! Everybody has got everything that can be thought of."

"Oh, no," said her confidential adviser, Miss Lester, in a soothing tone. "You have means of buying everything you can fancy; and when every shop and store is glittering with all manner of splendors, you cannot surely be at a loss."

"Well, now, just listen. To begin with, there's mamma. What can I get for her? I have thought of ever so many things. She has three card cases, four gold thimbles, two or three gold chains, two writing desks of different patterns; and then as to rings, brooches, boxes, and all other things, I should think she might be sick of the sight of them. I am sure I am," said she, languidly gazing on her white and jeweled fingers.

This view of the case seemed rather puzzling to the adviser, and there was silence for a few minutes, when Ellen, yawning, resumed:

"And then there's cousins Jane and Mary; I suppose they will be coming down on me with a whole load of presents; and Mrs. B. will send me something—she did last year; and then there's cousins William and Tom—I must get them something; and I would like to do it well enough, if I only knew what to get."

"Well," said Eleanor's aunt, who had been sitting quietly rattling her knitting needles during this speech, "it's a pity that you had not such a subject to practice on as I was when I was a girl. Presents did not fly about in those days as they do now. I remember, when I was ten years old, my father gave me a most marvelously ugly sugar dog for a Christmas gift, and I was perfectly delighted with it, the very idea of a present was so new to us."

"Dear aunt, how delighted I should be if I had any such fresh, unsophisticated body to get presents for! But to get and get for people that have more than they know what to do with now; to add pictures, books, and gilding when the centre tables are loaded with them now, and rings and jewels when they are a perfect drug! I wish myself that I were not sick, and sated, and tired with having everything in the world given me."

"Well, Eleanor," said her aunt, "if you really do want unsophisticated subjects to practice on,

48

*I can put you in the way of it. I can show you
more than one family to whom you might
seem to be a very good fairy, and where such
gifts as you could give with all ease would seem
like a magic dream."*

*"Why, that would really be worth while,
aunt."*

*"Look over in that back alley," said her
aunt. "You see those buildings?"*

"That miserable row of shanties? Yes."

*"Well, I have several acquaintances there
who have never been tired of Christmas gifts or
gifts of any other kind. I assure you, you could
make quite a sensation over there."*

"Well, who is there? Let us know."

*"Do you remember Owen, that used to make
your shoes?"*

"Yes, I remember something about him."

*"Well, he has fallen into a consumption, and
cannot work any more; and he, and his wife,
and three little children live in one of the
rooms."*

"How do they get along?"

*"His wife takes in sewing sometimes, and
sometimes goes out washing. Poor Owen! I was
over there yesterday; he looks thin and wasted,
and his wife was saying that he was parched
with constant fever, and had very little appetite.
She had, with great self-denial, and by
restricting herself almost of necessary food, got*

him two or three oranges; and the poor fellow
seemed so eager after them."

"Poor fellow!" said Eleanor, involuntarily.

"Now," said her aunt, "suppose Owen's wife
should get up on Christmas morning and find
at the door a couple of dozen of oranges, and
some of those nice white grapes, such as you
had at your party last week; don't you think it
would make a sensation?"

"Why, yes, I think very likely it might; but
who else, aunt? You spoke of a great many."

"Well, on the lower floor there is a neat little
room, that is always kept perfectly trim and
tidy; it belongs to a young couple who have
nothing beyond the husband's day wages to
live on. They are, nevertheless, as cheerful and
chipper as a couple of wrens; and she is up
and down half a dozen times a day, to help
poor Mrs. Owen. She has a baby of her own
about five months old, and of course does all
the cooking, washing, and ironing for herself
and husband; and yet, when Mrs. Owen goes
out to wash, she takes her baby, and keeps it
whole days for her."

"I'm sure she deserves that the good fairies
should smile on her," said Eleanor; "one baby
exhausts my stock of virtues very rapidly."

"But you ought to see her baby," said Aunt
E.; "so plump, so rosy, and so good-natured,
and always clean as a lily. This baby is a sort

51

of household shrine; nothing is too sacred or too good for it; and I believe the little thrifty woman feels only one temptation to be extravagant, and that is to get some ornaments to adorn this little divinity."

"Why, did she ever tell you so?"

"No; but one day, when I was coming down stairs, the door of their room was partly open, and I saw a peddler there with open box. John, the husband, was standing with a little purple cap on his hand, which he was regarding with mystified, admiring air, as if he didn't quite comprehend it, and trim little Mary gazing at it with longing eyes.

" 'I think we might get it,' said John.

" 'Oh, no,' said she, regretfully; 'yet I wish we could, it's so pretty!' "

"Say no more, aunt. I see the good fairy must pop a cap into the window on Christmas morning. Indeed, it shall be done. How they will wonder where it came from, and talk about it for months to come!"

"Well, then," continued her aunt, "in the next street to ours there is a miserable building, that looks as if it were just going to topple over; and away up in the third story, in a little room just under the eaves, live two poor, lonely old women. They are both nearly on to ninety. I was in there day before yesterday. One of them is constantly confined to her bed with

52

rheumatism; the other, weak and feeble, with failing sight and trembling hands, totters about, her only helper; and they are entirely dependent on charity."

"Can't they do anything? Can't they knit?" said Eleanor.

"You are young and strong, Eleanor, and have quick eyes and nimble fingers; how long would it take you to knit a pair of stockings?"

"I?" said Eleanor. "What an idea! I never tried, but I think I could get a pair done in a week, perhaps."

"And if somebody gave you twenty-five cents for them, and out of this you had to get food, and pay room rent, and buy coal for your fire, and oil for your lamp—"

"Stop, aunt, for pity's sake!"

"Well, I will stop; but they can't: they must pay so much every month for that miserable shell they live in, or be turned into the street. The meal and flour that some kind person sends goes off for them just as it does for others, and they must get more or starve; and coal is now scarce and high priced."

"O aunt, I'm quite convinced, I'm sure; don't run me down and annihilate me with all these terrible realities. What shall I do to play good fairy to these old women?"

"If you will give me full power, Eleanor, I will put up a basket to be sent to them that will

53

give them something to remember all winter."

"Oh, certainly I will. Let me see if I can't think of something myself."

"Well, Eleanor, suppose, then, some fifty or sixty years hence, if you were old, and your father, and mother, and aunts, and uncles, now so thick around you, lay cold and silent in so many graves—you have somehow got away off to a strange city, where you were never known—you live in a miserable garret, where snow blows at night through the cracks, and the fire is very apt to go out in the old cracked stove—you sit crouching over the dying embers the evening before Christmas—nobody to speak to you, nobody to care for you, except another poor old soul who lies moaning in the bed. Now, what would you like to have sent you?"

"O aunt, what a dismal picture!"

"And yet, Ella, all poor, forsaken old women are made of young girls, who expected it in their youth as little as you do, perhaps."

"Say no more, aunt. I'll buy—let me see—a comfortable warm shawl for each of these poor women; and I'll send them—let me see—oh, some tea—nothing goes down with old women like tea; and I'll make John wheel some coal over to them; and, aunt, it would not be a very bad thought to send them a new stove. I remember, the other day, when mamma was

54

*pricing stoves, I saw some such nice ones for
two or three dollars."*

*"For a new hand, Ella, you work up the idea
very well," said her aunt.*

*"But how much ought I to give, for any one
case, to these women, say?"*

*"How much did you give last year for any
single Christmas present?"*

*"Why, six or seven dollars for some; those
elegant souvenirs were seven dollars; that ring I
gave Mrs. B. was twenty."*

*"And do you suppose Mrs. B. was any
happier for it?"*

*"No, really, I don't think she cared much
about it; but I had to give her something,
because she had sent me something the year
before, and I did not want to send a paltry
present to one in her circumstances."*

*"Then, Ella, give the same to any poor,
distressed, suffering creature who really needs
it, and see in how many forms of good such a
sum will appear. That one hard, cold, glittering
ring, that now cheers nobody, and means
nothing, that you give because you must, and
she takes because she must, might, if broken
up into smaller sums, send real warm and
heartfelt gladness through many a cold and
cheerless dwelling, through many an aching
heart."*

"You are getting to be an orator, aunt; but

don't you approve of Christmas presents, among friends and equals?"

"Yes, indeed," said her aunt, fondly stroking her head. "I have had some Christmas presents that did me a world of good—a little book mark, for instance, that a certain niece of mine worked for me, with wonderful secrecy, three years ago, when she was not a young lady with a purse full of money—that book mark was a true Christmas present; and my young couple across the way are plotting a profound surprise to each other on Christmas morning. John has contrived, by an hour of extra work every night, to lay by enough to get Mary a new calico dress; and she, poor soul, has bargained away the only thing in the jewelry line she ever possessed, to be laid out on a new hat for him.

"I know, too, a washerwoman who has a poor lame boy—a patient, gentle little fellow —who has lain quietly for weeks and months in his little crib, and his mother is going to give him a splendid Christmas present."

"What is it, pray?"

"A whole orange! Don't laugh. She will pay ten whole cents for it; for it shall be none of your common oranges, but a picked one of the very best going! She has put by the money, a cent at a time, for a whole month; and nobody knows which will be happiest in it, Willie or

*his mother. These are such Christmas presents
as I like to think of—gifts coming from love,
and tending to produce love; these are the
appropriate gifts of the day."*

*"But don't you think that it's right for those
who* have *money to give expensive presents,
supposing always, as you say, they are given
from real affection?"*

*"Sometimes, undoubtedly. The Saviour did
not condemn her who broke an alabaster box
of ointment—very precious—simply as a proof
of love, even although the suggestion was
made, 'This might have been sold for three
hundred pence, and given to the poor.' I have
thought he would regard with sympathy the
fond efforts which human love sometimes
makes to express itself by gifts, the rarest and
most costly. How I rejoiced with all my heart,
when Charles Elton gave his poor mother that
splendid Chinese shawl and gold watch!
because I knew they came from the very
fulness of his heart to a mother that he could
not do too much for—a mother that has done
and suffered everything for him. In some such
cases, when resources are ample, a costly gift
seems to have a graceful appropriateness; but I
cannot approve of it if it exhausts all the
means of doing for the poor; it is better, then, to
give a simple offering, and to do something for*

those who really need it."

Eleanor looked thoughtful; her aunt laid down her knitting, and said, in a tone of gentle seriousness, "Whose birth does Christmas commemorate, Ella?"

"Our Saviour's, certainly, aunt."

"Yes," said her aunt. "And when and how was he born? In a stable! laid in a manger; thus born, that in all ages he might be known as the brother and friend of the poor. And surely, it seems but appropriate to commemorate his birthday by an especial remembrance of the lowly, the poor, the outcast, and distressed; and if Christ should come back to our city on a Christmas day, where should we think it most appropriate to his character to find him? Would he be carrying splendid gifts to splendid dwellings, or would he be gliding about in the cheerless haunts of the desolate, the poor, the forsaken, and the sorrowful?"

And here the conversation ended.

"What sort of Christmas presents is Ella buying?" said Cousin Tom, as the servant handed in a portentous-looking package, which had been just rung in at the door.

"Let's open it," said saucy Will. "Upon my word, two great gray blanket shawls! These

must be for you and me, Tom! And what's this?
A great bolt of cotton flannel and gray yarn
stockings!"

The door bell rang again, and the servant
brought in another bulky parcel, and deposited
it on the marble-topped centre table.

"What's here?" said Will, cutting the cord.
"Whew! a perfect nest of packages! Oolong tea!
oranges! grapes! white sugar! Bless me, Ella
must be going to housekeeping!"

"Or going crazy!" said Tom; "and on my
word," said he, looking out of the window,
"there's a drayman ringing at our door, with a
stove, with a teakettle set in the top of it!"

"Ella's cook stove, of course," said Will; and
just at this moment the young lady entered,
with her purse hanging gracefully over her
hand.

"Now, boys, you are too bad!" she
exclaimed, as each of the mischievous
youngsters was gravely marching up and
down, attired in a gray shawl.

"Didn't you get them for us? We thought you
did," said both.

"Ella, I want some of that cotton flannel, to
make me a pair of pantaloons," said Tom.

"I say, Ella," said Will, "when are you going
to housekeeping? Your cooking stove is
standing down in the street; 'pon my word,

John is loading some coal on the dray with it."

"Ella, isn't that going to be sent to my office?" said Tom; "do you know I do so languish for a new stove with a teakettle in the top, to heat a fellow's shaving-water!"

Just then, another ring at the door, and the grinning servant handed in a small brown paper parcel for Miss Ella. Tom made a dive at it, and tearing off the brown paper, discovered a jaunty little purple velvet cap, with silver tassels.

"My smoking cap, as I live!" said he; "only I shall have to wear it on my thumb, instead of my head—too small entirely," said he, shaking his head gravely.

"Come, you saucy boys," said Aunt E., entering briskly. "What are you teasing Ella for?"

"Why, do see this lot of things, aunt! What in the world is Ella going to do with them?"

"Oh, I know!"

"You know! Then I can guess, aunt, it is some of your charitable works. You are going to make a juvenile Lady Bountiful of El, eh?"

Ella, who had colored to the roots of her hair at the exposé of her very unfashionable Christmas preparations, now took heart, and bestowed a very gentle and salutary little cuff on the saucy head that still wore the purple cap, and then hastened to gather up her various purchases.

"Laugh away," said she, gayly; "and a good many others will laugh, too, over these things. I got them to make people laugh—people that are not in the habit of laughing!"

"Well, well, I see into it," said Will; "and I tell you I think right well of the idea, too. There are worlds of money wasted, at this time of the year, in getting things that nobody wants, and nobody cares for after they are got; and I am glad, for my part, that you are going to get up a variety in this line; in fact, I should like to give you one of these stray leaves to help on," said he, dropping a ten dollar note into her paper. "I like to encourage girls to think of something besides breastpins and sugar candy."

But our story spins on too long. If anybody wants to see the results of Ella's first attempts at good fairyism, they can call at the doors of two or three old buildings on Christmas morning, and they shall hear all about it.

GAMES, DANCES,
AND PANTOMIME

At Christmas play, and make good cheer,
For Christmas comes but once a year.
                                    Thomas Tusser

In Victorian times, Christmas festivities
continued for twelve days, during which the
Victorians especially enjoyed dances,
pantomime and parlor games. Dressing in
costume was also customary.

The old housekeeper had been consulted; the
antique clothes-presses and wardrobes
rummaged, and made to yield up the relics of
finery that had not seen the light for several
generations; the younger part of the company
had been privately convened from parlor and
hall, and the whole had been bedizened out,
into a burlesque imitation of an antique mask.
      from Washington Irving's *Old Christmas*

Games such as blind man's bluff and charades amused children and adults alike. Families also enjoyed going to the theater to see plays like *Puss in Boots, The Ogre of Rat's Castle, Harlequin,* or a Punch and Judy show.

As Twelfth Night approached, the dancing ceased, the decorations and greenery were put away, and the New Year began. Soon came the feast of Epiphany, commemorating the day on which the three wise men were guided by the star to the stable at Bethlehem.

"What means that star," the Shepherds said,
"That brightens through the rocky glen?"
And angels, answering overhead,
Said, "Peace on earth, good-will to men!"
James Russell Lowell

And "peace on earth, good will to men," is what we today still wish for all. As our beloved Victorian Charles Dickens wrote:

I will honor Christmas in my heart,
and try to keep it all the year.